2/95

DATE			

BAKER & TAYLOR

A Picture Book of
Sojourner Truth

David A. Adler

illustrated by Gershom Griffith

Holiday House/New York

Library of Congress Cataloging-in-Publication Data
Adler, David A.
A picture book of Sojourner Truth / by David A. Adler:
illustrated by Gershom Griffith. — 1st ed.
p.   cm.
Summary: An introduction to the life of the woman born into
slavery who became a well-known abolitionist and crusader for
the rights of African Americans in the United States.
ISBN 0-8234-1072-2
1. Truth, Sojourner, d. 1883—Juvenile literature.   2. Afro-
Americans—Biography—Juvenile literature.   3. Abolitionists—
United States—Biography—Juvenile literature.   4. Social
reformers—United States—Biography—Juvenile literature.
[1. Truth, Sojourner, d. 1883.   2. Abolitionists.   3. Reformers.
4. Afro-Americans—Biography.]   I. Griffith, Gershom, ill.
II. Title
E185.97.T8A35   1994   93-7478   CIP   AC
305.5′67′092—dc20
[B]

Other books in David A. Adler's *Picture Book Biography* series

A Picture Book of George Washington
A Picture Book of Abraham Lincoln
A Picture Book of Martin Luther King, Jr.
A Picture Book of Thomas Jefferson
A Picture Book of Benjamin Franklin
A Picture Book of Helen Keller
A Picture Book of Eleanor Roosevelt
A Picture Book of Christopher Columbus
A Picture Book of John F. Kennedy
A Picture Book of Simón Bolívar
A Picture Book of Harriet Tubman
A Picture Book of Florence Nightingale
A Picture Book of Jesse Owens
A Picture Book of Anne Frank
A Picture Book of Frederick Douglass
A Picture Book of Sitting Bull
A Picture Book of Rosa Parks
A Picture Book of Robert E. Lee

Sojourner Truth was born in 1797 in Hurley, New York. She was the daughter of slaves Betsey and James Hardenbergh.

Betsey and James's master was Colonel Johannes Hardenbergh, from whom Sojourner's parents took their family name.

Sojourner's father was also called Baumfree, the Low Dutch word for tree, because he seemed as mighty as one. Sojourner grew to look like him—tall, straight, and strong.

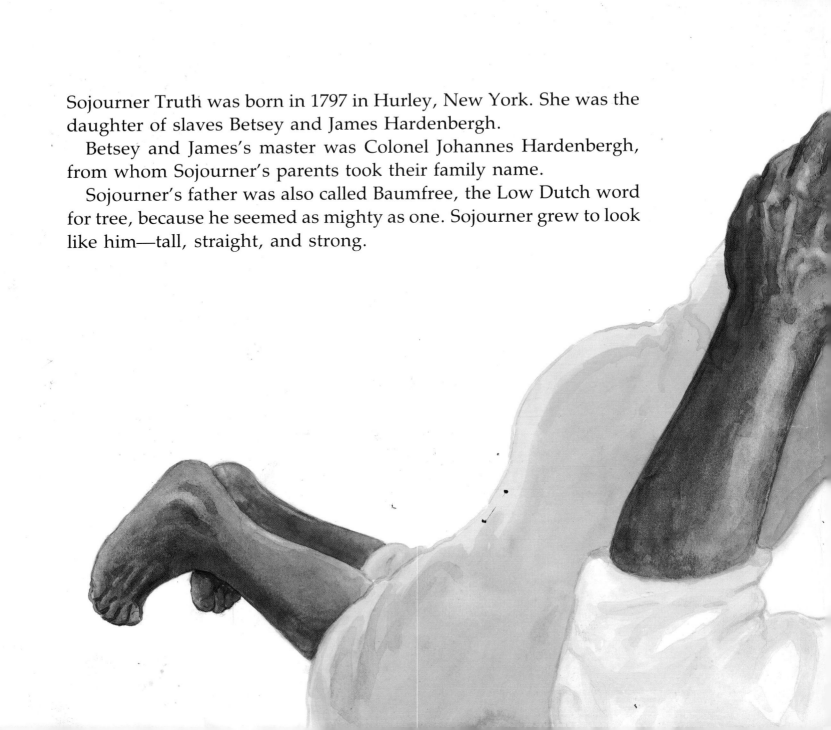

When Sojourner was born, her parents named her Isabella and called her Belle. Many years later, when she was a free woman, she renamed herself Sojourner Truth.

Isabella had many brothers and sisters, but most of them had been sold to slave traders and taken away before she was born. Sometimes at night her mother looked at the sky and sadly told Isabella, "Those are the same stars, and that is the same moon, that look down upon your brothers and sisters . . . though they are ever so far away from us and each other."

Isabella hated the way slavery tore families apart. "Oh, Lord," she said many years later, "what is this slavery that it can do such dreadful things?"

When Isabella was three, Johannes Hardenbergh died. His son, Charles, was her new owner. Isabella, her parents, and her younger brother Peter lived with other slaves in the cold, wet, one-room cellar of Charles Hardenbergh's house.

When Isabella was nine, she was taken from her family and brother and sold to Mr. and Mrs. John Neely, who beat her.

Isabella's mother had taught her to pray and believe in God. In her prayers Isabella begged for protection from the Neelys.

Two years later, Isabella was sold to Martin Schryver, a fisherman and innkeeper. After another year and a half, she was sold to John Dumont.

Isabella worked hard for the Dumonts. Her master boasted to his friends that she "will do a good family's washing in the night and be ready in the morning to go into the field, where she will do as much at raking and binding as my best hands."

While Isabella worked for the Dumonts, she met Robert, a slave who worked at a nearby farm. She said later that she truly loved him. One day his master and master's sons caught Robert visiting Isabella. They beat Robert severely with heavy sticks, tied him up, and took him away. After that Robert never came back.

Isabella later agreed to marry Thomas, a slave who worked for Dumont. It was a marriage encouraged by Dumont to increase the number of his slaves. Isabella and Thomas had five children together: Diana, Elizabeth, Hannah, Peter, and Sophia.

In 1817, a New York state law was passed that would grant freedom to Isabella and other slaves in ten years, on July 4, 1827. Dumont promised to free Isabella in nine years, on July 4, 1826, if she continued to work hard for him.

She worked in the fields planting, plowing, and harvesting, but when the time came for her release, John Dumont refused.

Isabella was furious. She decided to run away, but first she finished her work. She spun about one hundred pounds of her master's wool. Then, early in the morning, she took her infant daughter Sophia and left to find Levi Rowe, a farmer and Quaker who hated slavery. Isabella told him her story, and he sent her to Isaac and Maria Van Wagener.

Dumont found Isabella at the Van Wageners' and demanded that she come back.

"I won't," she said.

The Van Wageners then paid Dumont for Isabella and Sophia's freedom.

Isabella worked for the Van Wageners through the winter of 1826. Then, in 1827, she learned that her five-year-old son, Peter, had been sold by Dumont to Solomon Gedney who sold Peter to an Alabama planter. Such a sale, to someone outside New York State, was against the law.

Isabella told Mrs. Dumont, "I'll have my child again."

She went to court, sued Gedney, and won. She was one of the first African-American women in the United States to win a lawsuit against a white man.

In 1829, Isabella took Peter and moved to New York City, where she worked as a servant. Then, in 1833, she went north to Sing Sing, New York, and joined a religious community called the "Kingdom of God." She gave it all her money and did most of the work.

In 1834, the leader of the Kingdom died. Isabella was wrongly accused in a New York newspaper of poisoning him and trying to poison others, too. She sued the reporter for hurting her good name, and again she won. The newspaper and the man who gave the false story were ordered to pay Isabella $125.

Isabella returned to New York City and worked as a servant. But she was unhappy there and said, "The rich rob the poor and the poor rob one another." In June 1843, she told the woman for whom she worked that she was going west. "The Spirit calls me there," she said, "and I must go."

She also told the woman that she was no longer Isabella, but Sojourner, since she planned to sojourn, to move about and visit different places, and to preach. And since she considered God to be her only master, and his name was Truth, she called herself Sojourner Truth.

Sojourner's travels took her thousands of miles, across many states. She preached on religion, spoke out against slavery, and stood up for the rights of women. Her humor, common sense, and the power of her ideas made her one of the great speakers of her time.

Sojourner Truth could neither read nor write, but wherever she went, community and antislavery leaders came to hear her speak. She knew much of the Bible by heart. "I talk to God," she said, "and God talks to me."

A woman who heard her in Akron, Ohio, wrote later that Sojourner Truth "stood nearly six feet high, head erect, and eye piercing the upper air like one in a dream. At her first word there was a profound hush. She spoke in deep tones, which though not loud, reached every ear in the house."

Sojourner Truth called slave owners sinners who soon would be punished by God. She laughed at the idea that women were weaker than men. "Look at me," she said. "I have plowed and planted . . . and ain't I a woman?" She even pulled up her sleeve and showed the audience her muscular arm. "Sisters," she said, "if women want any rights, more than they got, why don't they just take them, and not be talking about it?"

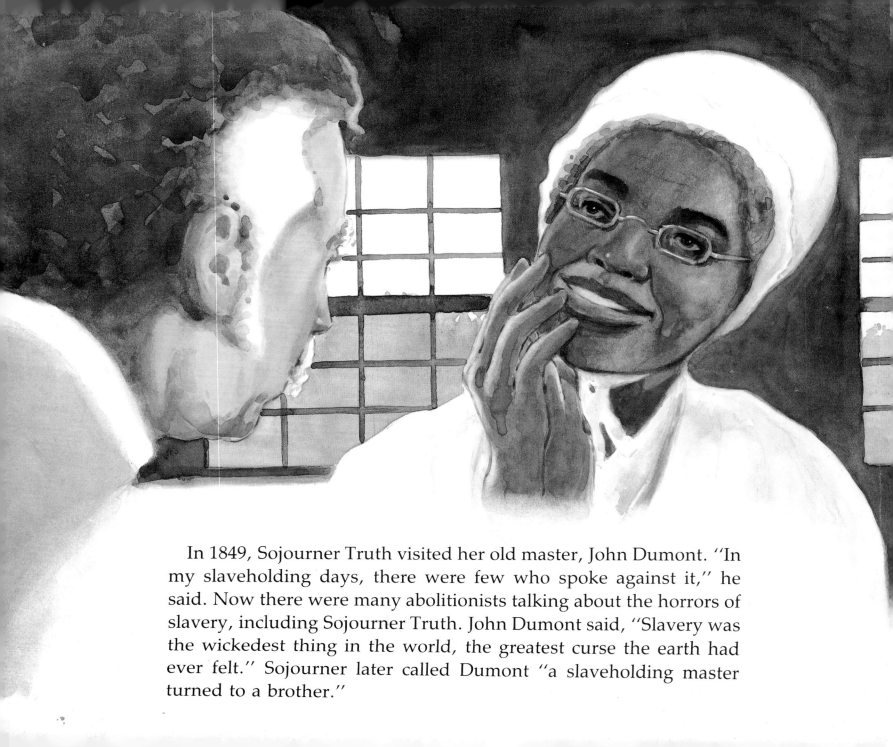

In 1849, Sojourner Truth visited her old master, John Dumont. "In my slaveholding days, there were few who spoke against it," he said. Now there were many abolitionists talking about the horrors of slavery, including Sojourner Truth. John Dumont said, "Slavery was the wickedest thing in the world, the greatest curse the earth had ever felt." Sojourner later called Dumont "a slaveholding master turned to a brother."

Sojourner Truth told the story of her life to her friend Olive Gilbert who wrote it down. In 1850, *The Narrative of Sojourner Truth* was published. The money Sojourner earned selling copies of her book helped support her while she traveled and spoke.

In 1857, Sojourner Truth bought a house near Battle Creek, Michigan. Some of her children and grandchildren moved there to be with her.

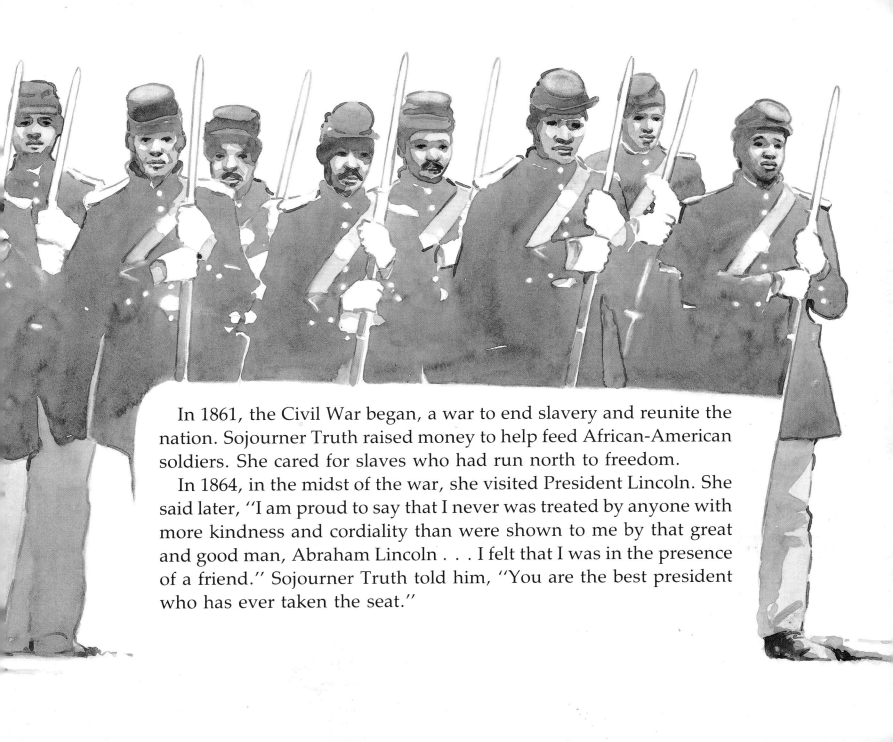

In 1861, the Civil War began, a war to end slavery and reunite the nation. Sojourner Truth raised money to help feed African-American soldiers. She cared for slaves who had run north to freedom.

In 1864, in the midst of the war, she visited President Lincoln. She said later, "I am proud to say that I never was treated by anyone with more kindness and cordiality than were shown to me by that great and good man, Abraham Lincoln . . . I felt that I was in the presence of a friend." Sojourner Truth told him, "You are the best president who has ever taken the seat."

When she came to Washington, D.C., slave traders were at work in nearby Maryland. Sojourner Truth gathered Union soldiers and together they chased away the slave traders.

In 1864, she was appointed as a counselor to the freed slaves at Arlington Heights, Virginia. She worked in the Freedman's Hospital, too.

At times, when she worked at the hospital, she rode in segregated, horse-drawn streetcars. Black people and white people were seated separately and often drivers would not even stop for African-Americans.

Sojourner Truth complained to the president of the streetcar company. He pledged to give blacks and whites equal privileges.

Then one day a streetcar driver refused to stop for her. She stood in front of the next streetcar to force that driver to stop. When she climbed aboard, the conductor told her, "Go forward where the horses are or I will throw you out." Sojourner Truth refused to sit there. She sat where she wanted.

When another conductor pushed her, she had him arrested. She said later that his trial created a great sensation. Before it ended, "the inside of the cars looked like pepper and salt." Blacks and whites were sitting together.

After the war ended, Sojourner Truth spoke to President Ulysses S. Grant and to Congress. She proposed that freed slaves be given western land so they could support themselves. Her plan was never adopted.

In the 1870s, many freed slaves were out of work and lived in terrible poverty.

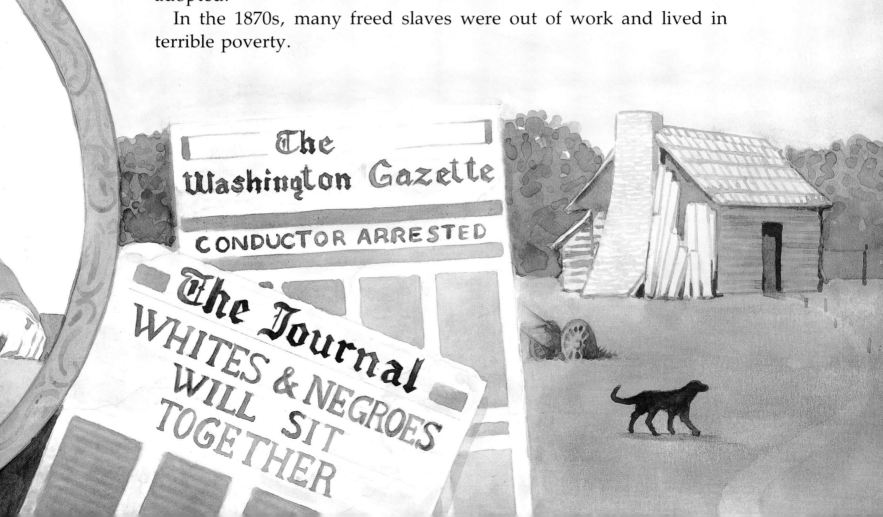

Sojourner Truth soon realized that freedom from slavery did not mean freedom from poverty, hatred, and discrimination.

Sojourner Truth had dreamed of equality for all people, black and white, male and female. When she died, on November 26, 1883, her dream had still not been fulfilled. But she was one of the brave, outspoken people who began the struggle.

AUTHOR'S NOTE

For most slaves, no record was kept of their birth, and the exact date of Sojourner Truth's is unknown. Even the year is not certain. Other dates as well, especially in Sojourner's early life, are not definite. My sources for many of the dates and much of the information included here were *The Narrative of Sojourner Truth*, her autobiography, first published in 1850, and *The Book of Life*, a collection of Sojourner Truth's letters and biographical sketches of her, first published in 1878.

In *Narrative* she referred to herself as Isabella before 1843, not Belle or Sojourner, so I did, too.

The first language Sojourner Truth learned was Low Dutch, spoken by her first master, Johannes Hardenbergh. She only learned English when she became the slave of John Neely.

Sojourner Truth carried a book in which she collected the autographs of the many great people she met. She said later that President Lincoln "took my little book, and with the same hand that signed the death-warrant of slavery, he wrote as follows: 'For Aunty Sojourner Truth, October 29, 1864. A. Lincoln.'"

To earn money while she gave free lectures, she sold pictures of herself with the caption, "I sell the shadow to support the substance. Sojourner Truth."

IMPORTANT DATES

1797	Born in Hurley, New York.
1806	Sold to John Neely.
1808	Sold to Martin Schryver.
1810	Sold to John Dumont.
1817	A New York state law was passed promising freedom on July 4, 1827, to all slaves born before July 4, 1799.
1826	Ran away from the Dumont farm.
1833–1834	Lived in Sing Sing, New York, at "the Kingdom of God." (Sing Sing became Ossining, New York, in 1901.)
1843	Left New York City, began her travels, and took the name Sojourner Truth.
1850	*The Narrative of Sojourner Truth* was published.
1852	Gave "Ain't I a Woman" speech in Akron, Ohio.
1857	Moved to Michigan.
1861–1865	The Civil War was fought.
1864	Met with President Abraham Lincoln.
1865	The Thirteenth Amendment to the U.S. Constitution freeing all slaves in the United States was ratified.
1870	Met with President Ulysses S. Grant.
1875	*The Book of Life* was published.
1883	Died in Battle Creek, Michigan, on November 26.

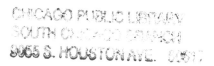